DIVORCING

A NARCISSIST

HOW TO END A DESTRUCTIVE MARRIAGE, PROTECT YOURSELF AND RECOVER AFTER A TOXIC RELATIONSHIP.

SIMON MACKENZIE

TABLE OF CONTENTS

INTRODUCTION

In the modern-day, we hear the word "narcissist" a lot, but how many of you actually understand the term? And how many of you have spent time with a narcissist?

It's very likely that having spent a reasonable amount of time with someone who calls into the narcissistic category, you quickly realize that this is someone who will either challenge you in ways you can't explain, or someone who you cannot handle being around for too long.

The problem is, not every repel narcissists easily. Some people find that they fall into the grips of a narcissist very easily, and it's only when their true nature reveals itself that they understand the true extent of the situation. By that time, however, it's usually very difficult to get away.

By the title of this book, you can tell that this guide is going to help you if you are thinking about divorcing the narcissist in your life. Whilst we're going to focus mostly on those who are married and seeking to end the union for good, there is some very actionable and pertinent advice for anyone who is currently in a relationship with a narcissist and wants to break free.

It's a sad truth that you are never going to be able to maintain a happy and fruitful relationship with a narcissist. This is not a healthy union, and it's one that will only damage you.

A narcissist doesn't feel love and empathy in the same way as those who aren't affected by this damaging personality disorder. Instead, they have no regard for the feelings of others.

Any relationship is hard, but when you're in a relationship with a narcissist, it's ten times harder. If you do find yourself married to someone who is either a total narcissist or someone who has distinct narcissistic tendencies, this isn't going to be a happy or healthy marriage. At some point, you might simply feel that you've had enough, you want to leave and you want to move on with your life and smile again, without feeling guilty for it.

Good for you.

When that moment comes, when that flashbulb goes off in your mind and you suddenly realize that you truly do deserve better, it's time to put the wheels of motion in action. However, it's essential to recognize that this isn't going to be easy.

Your feelings are involved. You married this person, so that must mean that you love them. While they're mistreating you now, it possibly wasn't always like that. Narcissists often display their very best behavior at the start of a relationship, showering you in charm and compliments. This is designed to get you where they want you, and the memory of this experience can often be enough to make you think that there's some good in there somewhere, when the bad behavior starts to show its ugly head.

Of course, divorce is not a decision anyone should take lightly, and it depends whether you share children as to whether extra steps need to be taken to ensure that nobody else is either damaged by the divorce or ends up feeling worse off in the end. For that reason, you need to know what you're facing, you need to know the steps you need to think about and take, and you need to understand that the whole experience will be tough, but worth it in the end.

That's where we come in.

This book is going to guide you through the whole process. From what you need to understand legally to what you need to realize emotionally, we've got you covered. That leaves you with the emotional time and freedom to focus on the other side of the story - the lasting effects that a relationship with a narcissist will have on you.

It's a sad end to a relationship that you probably hoped would last forever, but taking steps to free yourself from the grips of a narcissist is not a decision you will ever regret.

CHAPTER 1
WHAT IS A NARCISSIST?

Before we get into the specifics, we need to cover the basics.

Maybe you've picked up this book because you think that your partner might be a narcissist; you might have a few inklings that this could be the case, but you want to learn more to ensure whether or not this really is the case.

These first few chapters will give you all the background information you need to be able to either firmly state in your mind that you're dealing with a narcissist, or pass the idea off as something else entirely.

Information gives you power, and knowledge allows you to make solid and firm decisions that you're not always thinking back over and wondering whether you made the right choice.

When you choose to leave a narcissist, married or not, you're going to have times when you wonder whether you did the right thing or not. This is because you're going to be subjected to either a constant bombardment of charm, or you might end up with the opposite - a constant bombardment of blame and abuse. Depending upon which option you face, depends on how you feel during the process.

Remember, your mind is your own, even if the narcissist in your life tries to make you doubt it.

So, let's talk about what narcissism is and give you the background information you need to know.

Narcissistic Personality Disorder (NPD)

Narcissistic Personality Disorder, or NPD, is a recognized personality disorder that falls under the mental health spectrum or umbrella.

Whilst there are many people walking the streets who have very strong narcissistic traits, they may not meet all the criteria to be completely diagnosed with NPD itself. The issue is also complicated by the fact that most narcissists truly believe there is nothing wrong with them, so they're never going to reach out for help and will therefore never be diagnosed.

Can you see what we're dealing with here?

Many people who could easily enter your life and damage your emotions, because they have a condition which is not controlled, not diagnosed, and not understood.

There is no known cure for NPD. There are no medications a narcissist can take to change their behavior and there is no therapy they can do which will magically cure the problem. The only treatment option available is a long series of cognitive-behavioral therapy sessions which aims to help the individual face their character, challenge it, and rectify it over time. Even then, there is no guarantee that this therapy will have a long-lasting effect on the individual.

Again, this type of therapy for NPD is extremely rare in take-up, because most narcissists do not believe they need treatment. If anything, narcissists believe there is something wrong with you, and not them.

Of course, that's extremely far off the mark, but pushing that thought onto you is what they do best.

There are many different types of narcissists, and there are varying degrees of severity. You might meet someone who is a very mild narcissist, and you only really notice their behavior occasionally. However, you may also meet someone who is a full-blown, raging narcissist, and this is the type of person who you really cannot have a healthy or long-lasting relationship with. In addition, there are the very worst types of narcissists, who share some of the same traits with sociopaths and psychopaths. Whilst these are rare, it's important to be aware of them.

NPD is characterized by a severely inflated sense of self-importance. The person believes that they are the most important person on the planet, that their opinions are right and matter more than anyone else's and that their needs are far more vital than yours. They have a very strong need for attention and they display zero empathy or sympathy for other people.

A narcissist can do or say something truly horrible and not feel bad about it. They will not feel shame or regret, because those emotions are simply not in their scope of possibility. They will come over as extremely confident, or they may come over as very lacking in confidence; it really depends on the type of narcissist you're dealing with. However, regardless of how they appear, they're extremely vulnerable to any type of criticism and will twist words that make it look you've wronged them in some terrible way.

Being around a narcissist truly is like treading on eggshells on a constant basis. It can be exhausting, and that's the very least of your worries. The other emotional damage that can occur as a result of spending a large amount of time with a narcissist, especially when you're closely connected, is likely to be quite far-reaching.

A very common question that often crops up is this - is a narcissist simply a bad person?

Well, it's difficult to say, but remember, they are suffering from a deeper condition and a personality disorder, that dictates the way they think and act. It's very difficult to have sympathy for a narcissist once you've spent time with them, because of the way they make you think and feel. They're people that can turn on the charm in an instant, but when they show their negative side, it's not a pleasant thing to see.

So, whilst it might not be completely fair to say that all narcissists are generally bad people, we can say that the behavior they exhibit and the damage they cause is very bad indeed.

10 Signs of You're Dealing With a Narcissist

Let's look at ten signs that you might be dealing with a narcissist, so you can compare your current situation and work out what the problem at hand really is.

1 - An Inflated Sense of Self-Importance

One of the biggest signs of narcissism is a sense of grandiose self-importance. A narcissist believes that they are the center of the universe and should remain there. Everyone else should orbit around them.

If you're with someone who always has to be the one in the middle of everything, if they have an extreme sense of importance and superiority, which goes way beyond regular arrogance, the chances are that you're dealing with a narcissist.

A narcissist has a sense that they are special and their uniqueness can only really be perceived or truly understood by those who are also special. This means that most narcissists will tend to try and associate with people of high social standing, experts in their fields, popular people, etc.

Put simply: a narcissist believes these are better than everyone around them and they believe they deserve this to be recognized. Of course, the truth is that they're no better than anyone else and they don't deserve any special treatment, but if you attempt to show them this truth, they will react in an aggressive or passive-aggressive way.

2 - Everything is About Them

Trying to have a conversation with a narcissist about anything other than them is very difficult and probably impossible. If you try and talk about something, perhaps about your day or something you're worried about, they will find a way to turn that conversation around and make it about them, their day, their accomplishments, the compliments they received that day, and how wonderful they are. They're also likely to weave in there how lucky you are to them in your life, because that's something they truly believe at their very core.

Put simply, they are the star and everyone else orbits around them. So, if you have a bad day and you're reaching out to your partner for a little support, don't expect to get anything in return. You're not going to get a hug, or a "tell me about it", or anyone who sits and lends an ear in this case, you're going to get a deflected conversation which is all about them and does nothing for the way you're feeling.

Of course, this is likely to make you feel not listened to, not cared about, not supported, and it means you're going to be bottling up your feelings and your concerns in life, because you're not being supported by your partner. This can lead to feelings of resentment over time, but can also be very damaging for your own mental health, because keeping your feelings locked up inside can be very damaging over time. We all need a sounding board, and that should always be our partner. In a marriage with a narcissist however, this is not going to happen.

3 - They Have to Have The Best of Everything

In order to support their sense of importance, they have to have the very best of everything in order to back up their claims. This might be the latest iPhone, the best car, the fanciest house, the nicest clothes, and they won't really care what sacrifices you have to make as a couple for this to happen.

In some cases, a narcissist will attach themselves to the best-looking person as a partner, because they see this person as an extension of themselves, and almost as a trophy. In this case, they're not bothered about you as a person, your needs, likes, dislikes, dreams, or desires, and they're simply concerned with what having you in their life does for their image and how it projects out to other people.

A narcissist is likely to be very materialistic, and that means they're going to focus on things rather than the most important things in life, such as experiences, love, relationships and deeper fulfillment.

4 - You Cannot Argue With a Narcissist

It's impossible to have an argument with a narcissist because they will give you no chance to argue your point back. They will simply shut you down and tell you that you're wrong. Of course, this is likely to cause you to become extremely angry and annoyed, simply because you feel pushed away or not taken seriously.

Over time however, the danger is that a person in a relationship with a narcissist will stop even trying. They won't have the fire and passion within them anymore to argue when they know something isn't right, because they'll see no point in making the effort. The fight as gone out of them. In addition, they might also start to feel that they really are wrong and that the narcissist is the right one. This is when the narcissist's manipulation has really taken hold and becomes damaging to the individual concerned.

5 - They Live in a Complete Fantasy

A narcissist will not see the world in the same way that you do. It's almost as if they're in their own magical world, which nobody else can see or understand, but they will 100% believe that they're living that life and that they're the most important person in it.

You might find that stories are made up, fantasies even, and it all works to support the idea they have of themselves, the grandeur that they have in their own mind. This is likely to place them in the center of any success story, painting them as the most attractive person in the room and the one that everyone gravitates towards.

The reason narcissists do this is quite complex, but it's thought to be to try and protect them from the reality of the situation. Of course, narcissists aren't the most important people in the world and they're not the center of the universe. The fantasy world they live in protects them from the harsh reality that they would otherwise be subjected to if they didn't use this tactic.

At the heart of it, narcissists might come over as supremely confident, but they're actually the opposite. Deep down, they're very fragile in terms of their self-confidence and these fantasies help to protect them from the negative feelings that would almost certainly engulf them if they went down a different route.

As a result, if you point out to a narcissist that something they're saying isn't quite right or doesn't add up, you're likely to be met with a defense that is so fierce, there's no point even trying to continue with it. They may become aggressive, passive-aggressive, or even emotionally bullying in order to protect the carefully orchestrated fantasy they've built up.

6 - *You Have to Give them a Constant Drip of Praise*

A narcissist needs a steady flow of compliments and praise in order to keep them happy. If they don't get this, it's almost as if the world they've so carefully created around them starts to crumble and fall down.

Deep down, the narcissist knows this, so they will surround themselves with people who are always feeding their ego. In a marriage to a narcissist, it's likely that they've turned you into someone who gives compliments and praise on a regular basis. Their friends, should they have any, are also likely to be people who are always feeding their ego and building them, to help protect that deep down fragile ego.

A narcissist needs someone to tell them that they're right at all times. This isn't because they don't believe they're not, it's because they need affirmation constantly, feeding the personality disorder that they have.

If you dare to criticize a narcissist or even stop giving them quite so many compliments, they're likely to take this in a very negative way and start to act out. This could be in many different ways, but the most likely route is either a verbal outburst or the silent treatment.

7 - They Expect You to Treat Them as Though They Are Royalty

The sense of entitlement we've already talked about and the fact that they always think they're right means that a narcissist needs you to treat them as though they're are the highest-ranking royalty in the land. They expect this special VIP treatment at all times and if they don't get it, they will forcibly question why.

A narcissist needs their partner to cater to every single need, desire and whim they have, no questions asked. You do not have any other value or reason to be around, as harsh as it sounds, you are only there to cater to their needs, however unrealistic. If you happen to ask for something yourself, perhaps ask them to do something for you, it's not going to happen and you're likely to notice a retaliation, usually the silent treatment again, or a verbal outburst.

8 - They Feel No Shame or Guilt Over Hurting Other People

After an argument or any other type of confrontation, if you show any emotion, don't expect it to be met with a sympathetic response. A narcissistic can easily hurt someone and not feel the slightest bit of guilt or shame.

They do not possess empathy, which allows them to recognize the feelings of another person and as a result, the word "sorry" is never likely to be uttered by them in your household. The problem is, you might find yourself uttering it, simply because you falsely believe that you're the one in the wrong.

Narcissists have no problems with using other people or taking advantage of them, either for the sheer hell of it, or because they want something of their own from it. In some cases, this can be out of the simple need to control or hurt someone, but most of the time, it's likely to be something a narcissist does without even thinking about it. It doesn't occur to them that what they do might affect another person emotionally and cause hurt or distress, and they probably wouldn't care if it did.

9 - They Regularly Put Others Down, Bully And Generally Belittle People

If you happen to be out for dinner with your partner and they see someone in the street they don't like the look of, be prepared for a harsh remark. In addition, a narcissist has no problem with general bullying behavior, sarcastic remarks that put others down and generally belittling behavior. They don't find a problem with this, because they don't have the empathy to understand how it might affect another person.

It's very easy for a narcissist to feel like they're being threatened, usually by someone who is quite loud, confident, perhaps popular, or someone very successful. As a result, they're likely to try and befriend that person, to make it look like they're on the same level, but anyone else is likely to be passed away with contempt. That is however just one way of dealing with it; in some cases, a narcissist will feel so threatened or challenged by someone who they perceive to be of a higher level than them, that they will try and drag them down and belittle them.

10 - They Often Turn on The Charm Like a Light Switch

Reading all these signs of a narcissist might make a person who has never been affected by a narcissist wonder why it can even happen. But this last point is the main crux - a narcissist isn't like this all of the time. They're able to turn the charm on and off to the point where it's like the sun coming out from behind a dark cloud.

At the start, when you first meet a narcissist, they will probably be the most fun-loving, charming person you've ever come into contact with. They do this to try and snare you into their grip. They're not going to show their true selves until they've got you right where they want you. When they feel comfortable that you're under their spell and you're not going anywhere, they'll start to let their true nature shine through.

Then, when it looks like you're about to become sick of their treatment, they turn the charm back on again, to keep you where they want you. This cycle is likely to continue until you reach the point where you can't take anymore. This is often the reason why a person stays with a narcissist and doesn't walk away, and it's this tactic that keeps a person right where they are.

If you're someone who tries to see the best in people, which we assume you are, then you're always going to remember the times when the narcissist was nice to you and made you feel good. You know that capability is in there, so you hang around and wait for it. When it is shown to you, it's like the biggest of highs. However, what you don't realize is that the 'good side' is fake and all an illusion.

How many of those ten signs can you apply to your partner? Remember, we're all human and that means that sometimes we don't act in a way which we should. You might snap at someone close to you or make them feel bad, simply because you've had a bad day, but the difference between that type of situation and someone who is a narcissist is that you'll generally feel bad about it afterward and either apologize or try and make it up to them in other ways.

Don't simply assume that someone is a narcissist because they show one or two signs from that list. However, if you can agree with many, it's likely that you're dealing with someone who has narcissist tendencies to some degree.

MAIN TYPES OF NARCISSISTS

It's not easy to try and work out why some people are narcissists and others aren't. Of course, we know that Narcissistic Personality Disorder is a condition, but there are countless other theories, which swirl around the same subject. For instance, Freud put forth the idea that all children go through a stage of development which includes something called "primary narcissism". It is at this point in their lives that they haven't yet grasped the idea that people are separate, need to be respected, etc. However, as normal development continues, this idea disappears and the healthy ideas of an adult take over.

In addition, a lot of research has gone into different types of narcissists. It's important to know the main differences so you can learn more about the subject in general. This will help you in your situation because you'll have more solid information on which to base your final decision.

If you break it down, there are actually two main types of narcissists - vulnerable narcissists and grandiose narcissists, who are also sometimes referred to as invulnerable narcissists.

Vulnerable narcissists are hard to spot because they don't come over as overly confident and if anything, they can seem shy. However, underneath it all, it can be quite a different story.

Vulnerable narcissists often have deep-seated feelings of loathing and in order to cover those up, they tend to create an illusion or impression of themselves which deflects how they really feel. They connect with those in power or those they assume to be more popular and they have no problem in stamping over anyone to be connected.

As with most types of narcissists, vulnerable narcissists don't care about the feelings of other people and have a total lack of empathy. One of the key tactics this type of narcissist uses is emotional manipulation, with gaslighting being the most common route. This helps to get the "you poor thing" type of sympathy they need to feel better about themselves and deal with their low self-worth.

On the other hand, the grandiose narcissist or invulnerable narcissist is the most common type and the one that you will associate the most with the picture of a narcissist. This person thinks they're better than everyone else, dresses to impress and doesn't care who they hurt. They're very confident, and don't display the same low self-worth that a vulnerable narcissist does. If anything they have a very thick skin!

Within these two main types however, there are a few smaller groups to discuss, and it's these subtypes which allow you to really pinpoint the type of narcissist you're dealing with.

Amorous Narcissism - This type of narcissist focuses on attracting as many people as possible, usually has many one night stands, and doesn't care who knows about it.

Their level of self-worth is reflected in the number of people they sleep with and they're usually extremely charming, to get people to fall under their spell. You'll often hear of amorous narcissists being referred to as 'heartbreakers', because not only are they extremely charming and usually very well dressed/well turned out, but they don't care who they hurt in the end.

Compensatory Narcissism - This type of narcissist is trying to cover up or forget something which has happened to them in the past, possibly in their childhood. They'll usually create an image that is a total fantasy and they may appear completely overconfident. This type of narcissist is likely to prey on those who are shy or emotionally weaker, and is usually quite drawn to empaths too. Emotional manipulation is very commonly used by a compensatory empath.

Elitist Narcissism - This type of narcissist has to be the very best of everything, they have to have everything and they have to be the most well known. They will tread on anyone in order to get where they want to be, and they do not care who they hurt along the way. They are usually associated with others who are high up in their profession, simply because they've identified them and made sure that they become connected.

Malignant Narcissism - This type of narcissist is without a doubt the most dangerous to be around and if you do come into contact with this type of person, you need to get out of the situation as quickly as possible. This narcissist is dangerous, hurtful and very damaging and can often share the same traits as a sociopath or psychopath. This narcissist has zero care for feelings and doesn't understand morals. They have no care for remorse and they sometimes even feel delighted at the hurt they cause. Malignant narcissists are often in trouble with the law, more often than not.

As we begin to learn more about narcissism in general, there are sure to be more labels placed on different types. For now however, we know the basic traits that make up a narcissist person, regardless of the type that you want to call them. Can you identify your partner in this list?

POINTS TO REMEMBER FROM THIS CHAPTER

This chapter has been quite a lengthy one, but it's necessary in order for you to be able to understand the basics of narcissism for yourself.

You cannot make a decision about leaving your partner or divorcing them if you don't really understand the issue at hand. Hopefully, this chapter will have cleared your mind about narcissism and made you realize that the problem really does lie with them, and not you.

In our next chapter, we're going to talk about the reasons why the future with a narcissist is not at all bright and we're also going to cover some of the common emotional manipulation techniques that are used by these types of people. You've no doubt heard of 'gaslighting' before, and this falls into the emotional manipulation category with narcissists in a big way. We'll cover that in more detail shortly.

The main points to take from this chapter are:

- Narcissism is categorized at its core by an extremely inflated sense of self-importance and a total lack of empathy for other people;

- Narcissistic Personality Disorder (NPD) is very often undiagnosed, simply because the person doesn't believe there is anything wrong with them (a sign of narcissism) and therefore never reach out for help;

* Treatment for NPD is very limited and relies upon behavior changes and rewiring the brain to think in a different way. Even if treatment is taken up, the chances of success aren't guaranteed ;

* There are many different types of narcissists, but the most dangerous type is a malignant narcissist, who often shares traits with sociopaths and psychopaths ;

* A narcissist does not care about your feelings and only cares about the things you can do for them and how you make them look;

* Learning to identify accurately whether or not your partner is a narcissist is the first step towards freeing yourself from a potentially very damaging situation.

CHAPTER 2
WHY THE FUTURE WITH A NARCISSIST WILL NEVER BE BRIGHT

This chapter is designed to give you an idea of what the future will look like if you stay in the station you are in now. This chapter isn't meant to scare or upset you in any way, but it is designed to show you an honest picture of your potential future.

The fact that you are even questioning your relationship should be a red flag, but look within and think about the way you feel when you're subjected to the emotional abuse your partner no doubt uses upon you if they are indeed a narcissist.

Remember, narcissism is still narcissism, whether it's mild, moderate or severe, and it still hurts when your partner calls you names, belittles you, makes you feel like you're going crazy, or basically acts like they have no regard for your feelings. You do not have to live that way, and you should not live that way. You deserve better and you can get better, but first, you need to make the brave step to leave.

If you're on the fence about the whole thing and you're still not sure, let's look at why the future with a narcissist is never going to be the happy one you're dreaming of.

THE RELATIONSHIP IS AN ILLUSION

The sad truth is that the relationship you're in isn't actually a relationship. It cannot be, because a relationship is a mutual love and respect for each other. There is no mutual love in a narcissistic relationship and there is no mutual respect. Everything is one-sided.

You probably fell in love with your partner at the start because of the charm they showed you, the so-called good side they let you into and the worries and secrets they shared with you. It might be upsetting and hurtful to say this, but those worries and secrets were probably lies, and the so-called good side they showed you was nothing more than an act.

Narcissists are known for turning on the charm like a light switch and if you constantly hang on to the memories of when your partner showed you a sensitive, loving side, you're hanging onto something that is fake, completely not real.

You cannot have a healthy relationship with someone who doesn't care if you're hurt or not. You cannot have a healthy relationship with someone who doesn't feel empathy. Empathy is one of the vital cornerstones of a healthy relationship and without it, it's basically two people living side by side and not really caring what the other one thinks or feels.

The vows you gave at your wedding, if you had one, are nothing more than a one-sided sham.

Again, that sounds harsh, but it's the truth of the situation.

You will never be happy because your needs are not being met. Your partner doesn't care about your dreams, the bad day you had, the way you feel after they shout at you, or anything else that is related to your feelings; they only care about the things you can do for them and the way you can make others look at them.

That isn't the basis of any relationship, and it's not something you should stand for any longer.

If you want to be happy, and we hope that you do, then you need to break free, be brave, understand the situation, forgive yourself, and move on. Later on in the book, we're going to hold your hand and guide you through the whole thing.

The problem is, many people who have been subjected to the emotional abuse of a narcissist don't actually realize that they've been emotionally abused in the first place. This is the sign that a narcissist has done a very "good" job, because they've got to the point where their partner doubts their own sanity. For them, this is the outcome they want - now they have you right where they want you.

Let's explore a few common manipulation tactics used by narcissists, so you can identify whether or not you've been at the mercy of these in the past.

COMMON MANIPULATION TACTICS USED BY A NARCISSIST

Without a doubt, the single most common manipulation tactic used by a narcissist is gaslighting, but you might also notice passive-aggressive behavior too, as well as isolating the victim from those close to them.

Let's explore these three common tactics in this section.

Gaslighting

Gaslighting is a form of emotional manipulation and abuse, and it involves making the individual doubt their own sanity. An example of gaslighting might look a little like this:

You and your partner have a conversation before work and you agree to go to your favorite Italian restaurant after work to celebrate the fact that you're up for a promotion at work. You're really excited about the idea of being promoted and you've tried to talk to your partner about it many times, but you've been met with radio silence or a lack of interest. So, the idea that they want to take you out after work and celebrate is fantastic, giving you a warm glow all day.

After work, you go to the restaurant and wait outside as instructed, but your partner doesn't turn up. Instead, you're stood there for half an hour on your own.

You call your partner and ask where they are and they tell you they're at home. You mention the arrangements you know you had, but they tell you that you're making it up, you never agreed to go to the restaurant, and they throw in a remark about your promotion saying that they wouldn't go out to celebrate it yet anyway because it's not happened and probably won't.

You're upset and you start to question whether or not you really did arrange to meet, or whether you dreamed it. Your partner seemed very insistent that you never made those arrangements, and you're questioning yourself, searching your memory.

This is gaslighting.

Your partner did agree to meet you and they're using the fact that you might be promoted at work as a way to drag you down. They do not want you to be promoted because that's a success for you and it means they're not the center of the universe for a second. In addition, they're gaslighting by telling you that you're dreaming something, that you never arranged it, when deep down you know you did. This causes an internal conflict in your brain, questioning your own judgment and sanity.

The more this type of manipulation occurs, the more severe the effects become. Over time you start to seriously think you might be going crazy because these types of situations keep happening. However, deep down, you know that you're not wrong, and the conflict continues to rage.

Gaslighting of any type, over any period of time and to any severity, is a form of emotional abuse and it is one which is very commonly used by narcissists of all types.

You can find more information about this manipulation technique in my book "*Gaslighting: How to Recognize Hidden Behaviors of an Emotional Manipulator, Disarm the Narcissist and Find Healing after Psychological Abuse*".

Passive Aggressive Behavior

Another common manipulation tactic used by narcissists is the use of passive-aggressive behavior. Whilst this might seem like something everyone does occasionally, narcissists tend to take it to another level and use this type of behavior as a way of 'getting back' at someone, or causing them to feel bad about something they've said or done.

Giving someone the 'cold shoulder' or silent treatment is a common passive-aggressive tactic, but also backhanded and sarcastic remarks, quick outbursts followed by more silent treatment, etc. Aggressive behavior is different because it's direct and very easy to spot, but passive-aggressive behavior is a little harder to identify and it's more damaging emotionally because it causes the person it is aimed at to feel guilt or shame for whatever has caused the outburst/silent treatment.

The narcissist will often sulk or stare into space when acting in a passive-aggressive way, causing you to constantly ask 'what's wrong'. Of course, that will be met with either a sarcastic common or complete silence.

As with gaslighting, passive-aggressive behavior is a way of controlling someone by making them feel bad. In this case, unlike gaslighting, the narcissist isn't getting the person to doubt their own sanity or question their mind, but it's simply about making them feel guilty for something that the narcissist perceives them to have done wrong.

Of course, nine times out of ten, the person who the behavior is aimed towards has done nothing wrong, probably other than speaking the truth or their mind. To a narcissist however, this is simply not acceptable and it will be punished by using manipulation such as this as a control method.

The risk of passive-aggressive behavior is one of the reasons why being in a relationship with a narcissist is often about treading on eggshells. You will become fearful of experiencing this type of behavior, ,so you will modify your attitude and what you say and do to avoid this happening. Of course, that means you're censoring yourself and holding back, being fearful of the ramifications of doing something that is perfectly normal and acceptable in a regular relationship.

Social Isolation

Another common tactic is social isolation. This actually ties into the gaslighting side of things, but a narcissist is likely to try and pull their victim away from their regular support network, e.g., close friends and family.

They will try their very best to pull you away from those close to you by making you think that they don't care or they don't believe you, or maybe even think you're crazy. You'll notice small remarks such as "your friend doesn't really care about you anyway", or "they think you're overreacting all the time" and the more they say these things, the more the words start to seep into your subconscious, making you believe them over time.

Your friends and family are also more likely to be the ones who see the narcissistic behavior aimed at you and perhaps try and warn you. .As a result, you will be torn between believing them and wanting to stay by the side of your narcissist. The remarks the narcissist is sending your way will mean that you eventually start to separate from those close you, leaving you isolated and completely at the mercy of the abuse that is thrown your way.

Of course, in the end, your close friends and family will always be there for you and if you reach out and explain how you're feeling, it's very likely that they will come to your aid. However, in the meantime, you're likely to pull yourself away to the point where you're left alone, with only your narcissist for company. You will feel distrustful of anyone else as a result and that can seriously lower your self-esteem, your self worth, and your mood in a big way.

EMOTIONAL DAMAGE CAUSED BY A NARCISSIST

It's not rare for someone who has just come out of a relationship with a narcissist to need emotional support. This can either be from friends and family, or perhaps even professional help. If this is the case, take all the help you can get.

There is no shame in admitting that perhaps you're struggling and the degree of abuse that has been sent your way is quite likely to leave you feeling like you can't trust anyone. It's also very likely that a person who has been subjected to emotional abuse is going to struggle with entering into new relationships in the future.

It's important to take your time, heal in your own way and accept help and support whenever you feel you need it. In the case of divorcing a narcissist, you not only have to deal with the fact that your marriage has broken down beyond repair, the divorce proceedings you're going through and the emotional fall out from all of that, but the lasting effects of the emotional damage the narcissist has subjected you to. Some people don't even realize the degree to which they were struggling until after they've broken free.

Narcissistic victim syndrome is a common occurrence in people who have been in relationships with someone with narcissism. This is the lasting psychological and emotional effects which occur after the break up, including the possibility of flashbacks, PTSD, panic attacks, anxiety and associated depression.

Everyone is different, and everyone will feel that they need different levels of support. What is important however is that you don't avoid asking for help or taking help that is offered, simply because you think you can handle it or you're scared of what people might think of you. You have been through a tough time and you need to give yourself the tools to deal with it.

Dealing with a marriage breakdown and subsequent divorce is hard enough. This is one of the main causes of depression and anxiety overall, but when you add emotional abuse effects onto it, help and support will be needed to help you not only forgive yourself and realize that you did nothing wrong, but also to help you trust yourself again, before trying to trust anyone else.

POINTS TO REMEMBER FROM THIS CHAPTER

This chapter has focused on the emotional abuse which a narcissist often uses to control their victims. Again, this is about giving you the background information in order to make a sensible and healthy decision for your future.

Your relationship has no future. Sorry, but it's true. You cannot live a happy and healthy life in a relationship with a narcissist, let alone a marriage. There will come a point where you simply can't take it anymore and you either walk away or commit yourself to a life of misery. You do not deserve a life of misery.

The main points to take from this chapter are:

- A relationship and marriage with a narcissist is not a happy or healthy one;

- Your relationship is likely to be extremely one sided;

- Narcissists use various different manipulation tactics to get you where they want you and exert the control they crave as part of their personality disorder;

- Gaslighting, passive aggressive behavior and social isolation are the three main manipulation tactics a narcissist will use, but that doesn't mean they will be the only tactics that come your way;

- A narcissist will prey on your emotions, simply because they don't recognize their own and therefore don't have the empathy to understand when their words and actions may be causing distress;

- Dealing with the stress and worry of a divorce is known to be hard, however when you add dealing with the fall out of emotional abuse on top of that, you're looking at a difficult picture. With that in mind, you should accept any help and support offered to you and seek it out if you're struggling.

CHAPTER 3

5 REASONS WHY YOU'RE MAKING THE RIGHT DECISION

Up to now we've concentrated on the background to narcissism. We've done this because in order to make a solid and healthy decision, you need to be in possession of all the facts.

By this point you should be pretty clear on the picture of narcissism and why there isn't much hope for your relationship. It sounds harsh to say such things, but we want you to make a decision that is right for one, you one which will allow you to flourish and break free from damaging patterns and emotional abuse.

By this chapter, you might be still on the fence. You want to go, you want to feel better and look forward to a brighter future, but you're not 100%

sure. You love this person, you are married to them and it could be that you share things, such as a house and material items, and you might even have children.

In that case, you have to be very certain in your decision to divorce your narcissist and move forward in your life. This chapter is going to give you five final reasons why you are making the right decision by doing this. After that, if you choose to move forwards, we're going to get practical. We're going to talk you through, step by step, what you need to know and what you need to do in order to get the divorce ball rolling and the differences that you might encounter when a narcissist is involved in the whole process.

With that in mind, let's run through five reasons why divorcing a narcissist is the best idea.

Reason 1 - You Deserve Happiness

Why do you feel like you deserve to be beaten down every day of your life? Why do you deserve to be living through a rollercoaster of emotions every single day? Do you believe that you deserve to be controlled and manipulated?

It's very unlikely that you can, hand on heart, say that you're happy in your relationship. You might have convinced yourself that you are, and when your narcissist is happy and showing you the attention that you crave, you probably are, but it doesn't last, right? The highs are high and the lows are very low.

You do not have to live with this constant up and down pattern, you can be happy on an even level. Sure, nobody is happy all the time, but it's not normal to be so up and down through the space of a day.

Taking the brave decision to break away from your narcissistic marriage and seek a final divorce will allow you to seek closure. You will be able to seek out the support you need to overcome the lasting effects of the emotional abuse you've been subjected to, you and can look forward to a brighter future as a result.

Reason 2 - Children Within a Narcissistic Marriage Are Affected

If you have children, you need to be very aware of the effect this is having on them. Children will assume that this is a normal pattern of behavior and will go on to copy it in their future relationships. It's also possible that they're being subjected to emotional abuse on a different level, simply because your narcissistic partner doesn't have the empathy to show them love as they deserve and need.

If you want a real push in the right direction, if you want a good reason to leave, do it for your children, if you have them. You cannot raise healthy children in a marriage that is one part narcissist. There will be lasting effects, and whether they're mild or not, they're still effects that your children don't deserve to be subjected to.

You might think your children are happy and they probably are, but they're not being shown a healthy relationship between their parents. This will move into their future and cause them to act in ways which are unfair and unnecessary to their future partners.

If nothing else, do it for your children and their future.

Reason 3 - Your Mental Health is Suffering

Being subjected to emotional abuse on any level affects your self esteem, your self worth, and it affects your mental health. This leads you down a very dark and dangerous path which could put your overall wellbeing at risk.

It's quite common for the survivors of narcissistic abuse to have some amount of mental health damage when they break free. Those who stay in these types of unions are running the risk of serious problems, with depression and anxiety, stress, and even PTSD after the event becoming a reality.

Of course, we all have mental health, just as we all have physical health, but we don't tend to do things which endanger our physical health. With that in mind, why would you do something which would endanger your mental health?

It's time to place more importance on mental health overall and recognize the very damaging effects that problems such as being subjected to emotional abuse over a period of time can do.

Reason 4 - The Relationship Has no Future

In our very first chapter, giving you the basics of narcissism, we talked about the treatment options for a narcissist. They available treatment options might as well be zero, simply because they're extremely rarely taken up by narcissists, and even then, there's no guarantee that it will work.

With that in mind, your relationship is never going to change. He or she is not going to be cured, they're not going to change, they're not suddenly going to stop treating you badly or making you feel like everything is your fault and it's literally going to stay this way for the rest of your lives together.

Do you want that?

Be honest. Of course you don't.

This relationship does not have a future. Sure, it has some sort of future, but it won't be a happy or healthy one. Again, going back to our first reason, you deserve better, and whether you love this person or not (and we're assuming you do), sometimes you just have to hold your hands up and give up, say you gave it your best shot and walk away. It's the best option in the end.

Reason 5 - Relationships Aren't About Control

The final reason is to know what a real relationship is and what it feels like and looks like. A truly healthy and happy relationship doesn't have a requirement to control the other person within it. A narcissist has a need to control, they have to be the one holding the reins to everything because that way they can steer everything to make themselves look better than everyone else.

Healthy relationships allow each partner the space to grow and develop themselves, whilst being part of a partnership which allows them to flourish as people. This isn't possible in a narcissistic relationship because everything is one sided. You will never feel able to follow your dreams and be supported, you will always be dragged down. This means your life will never be fulfilling and you'll come to regret the time you wasted.

Break free from the control and look forward to a better life. The only way you can do that is by leaving the relationship and ending it for good. Yes, divorce is hard and you might not know where to start the whole process, but there is a lot of help and support out there and there are even legal professionals who have experience in dealing with divorces with narcissistic partners. Of course, we're also going to help you with all the advice we impart upon you throughout this book.

POINTS TO REMEMBER FROM THIS CHAPTER

This has been our final background information chapter and in some ways, a bit of a pep talk. You might have been a little on the fence about whether or not you're making the right decision and that's quite common. You've been subjected to abuse that has made you question your own sanity and you've been manipulated to the point of control. Of course you're going to question your decisions.

However, this is one decision that you're going to get right.

The main points to take from this chapter are:

- It's normal to doubt your decision to leave, but that doesn't mean you're making the wrong choice;

- A relationship with a narcissist will never change, because it's not possible to cure or change a narcissist;

- If you have children with your partner, they will be affected by the narcissism they're seeing directed towards you;

- You deserve happiness and a relationship that isn't dictated by control and one-sidedness.

Chapter 4

DIVORCING A NARCISSIST

Point 1 - Be Firm in Your Decision

Now we're moving on to the practical side of the book. By reaching this stage of the book it's likely that you've decided that you're right in your choice to divorce the narcissist in your life and you're ready to start the process.

That's good news, and you can be assured that it's a decision that will serve you well in years to come. For now however, it's vital that you understand what is in front of you, and before you get to that point, you need to be very firm in your choice and your decision.

If you're not sure of your choice or if you're wavering, you're more likely to give in to the continued manipulation and demands of the narcissist. As we'll explore as we move through these steps, it's very unlikely that your partner is going to just accept the decision and make life easier. If anything, they're likely to do everything to make it harder, because they will take your choice to divorce them as a serious personal dig, something that they just can't handle. That means, your decision has to be a solid one, to avoid you changing your mind when a little pressure comes your way.

It's not going to be easy, but it will be worth it in the end.

ASSESS THE SITUATION CAREFULLY

We've given you a lot of information so far about narcissism and the aim of that was to help you compare the picture of a narcissist with the situation you're in now. For sure, everyone is a little different and that means your situation might not fit the description we've given completely, but you will see similarities.

That is the whole point of this first section of the book - to give you peace of mind that you're right, that you're not going crazy, that you don't have to deal with this and that if you want to divorce your partner because you're simply not happy, you're perfectly within your rights to do so.

However, that doesn't mean you should take the decision lightly.

Ending a marriage, any marriage, is difficult and you need to be very sure that you're making the right choice for you. Starting divorce proceedings and then stopping them halfway through is not only distressing and upsetting for all involved, but it's also likely to cost you a fair amount of money in legal fees. In addition, starting divorce proceedings and then changing your mind is not sending the right message to your narcissistic partner.

They will take this as a win, that they've controlled you and changed your mind. They might turn on the charm for a while, keeping you right where they want you and making sure that you don't get any ideas about leaving again, but after a while, everything will just go back to the way it was before, if not worse. They now have this episode to throw at you during moments of manipulation.

So, when you decide to start divorcing your partner, you have to be sure that it's what you want and it's the decision you're going to move forwards with, no matter what.

Be rock sure and steady in your choice. It's normal to have moments of worry, but that doesn't mean you should change your mind.

ADOPT A POSITIVE MINDSET

Use every single part of your being to try and create a positive mindset. It can be hard in the circumstances but you have to try your best and focus on a brighter future. This will help you to overcome the difficulties that can arise when going through any type of divorce.

Divorcing your partner isn't just a case of "I don't want this anymore", it's a long and arduous process of unpicking the reasons why the relationship has failed, going through the necessary legal processes, splitting all belongings and coming to agreements. In the normal run of things, that can be very hard and very emotional, especially when there are still residual feelings in place. However, when you are divorcing a narcissist, it can be harder simply because trying to divide everything and come to agreements is borderline impossible without medical help.

Knowing this means that you're not going to have any nasty surprises. If you need to come up with a positive affirmation to use wherever things get tough, go do. Put into place mechanisms to help you feel positive and uplifted, whether that's heading out for a run whenever you feel like stress is starting to overwhelm you or simply focusing on your own self care. It's likely to feel odd at first, focusing on yourself, because you've been so used to being denied this basic right for so long. However, go with it and understand that it's your need and your right to look after yourself.

Move Forwards With Purpose

Once you're sure that you want to go down this route, you've tried your best to be as positive about it as possible, move forwards with purpose. Keep your eyes on the prize, i.e. that brighter future, and push through the hardships that will come your way.

We're not attempting to make this sound harder than it is, but we want you to be prepared for the reality of divorce, not least divorcing a narcissist. Put a plan together and work through it slowly and methodically. The rest of the information we're going to give you in this book will give you the information to do just that.

POINTS TO REMEMBER FROM THIS CHAPTER

This chapter has been the first one in your step by step guide to divorcing a narcissist. This chapter is about being very sure in your decision, because without that foundation your future happiness will remain very unsure. Cancelling divorce proceedings halfway through is not a good idea, not least for your bank account.

The main points to take from this chapter are:

- You need to be sure in your decision before you start divorce proceedings;

- Reading the informational chapters before will help you understand whether or not you really are affected by narcissism;

- Unfortunately, divorcing a narcissist is a long and arduous road and one which is likely to be difficult at some point. Being as positive as possible will allow you to see the process through;

- Once you're sure of your choice, you must move forwards with strength and purpose.

CHAPTER 5:

DIVORCING A NARCISSIST

POINT 2 - KNOW WHAT IS IN FRONT OF YOU

You've made your decision and you're sure divorce is what you want. Now, you need to do your research and know what is in front of you.

Your road throughout this divorce journey will be unique and will vary from person to person. Everyone has different situations and circumstances and that means your specifics will be unique. If you have children together, your divorce is likely to be a little more difficult, compared to someone who doesn't have children. However, that doesn't make it any less painful.

It's vital that you make a plan in terms of your finances and where you're going to live, and be prepared for whatever else may be thrown at you.

This chapter is going to talk about some of the situations that you need to focus on and some of the problems that might come your way. If you don't have children, the process of dividing up your belongings could be very difficult indeed, and if you own a house together, all of that needs to be dealt with.

You need to be sure that you can cope financially and you have a plan to help you through the difficult initial stages. You also need to know that your narcissist is not likely to behave well throughout this process. The fact you are divorcing them is a real kick in the teeth to them, and they're going to take it extremely personally, viewing it as a stain on their character. They will throw everything at you in order to punish you for this and also to turn everyone's attention back onto them, viewing them as the hero in the story.

This chapter is going to help you with all of that and highlight a few specifics.

EXPECT THE WORST

We've all heard the old 'expect the worst, hope for the best' line and that's what you need to do during a divorce of this kind. You need to realize that your narcissist is not going to play fair or kind. They're going to throw everything at you, they're going to make you look like the bad one and you're going to have to convince everyone around you that you're not the one in the wrong. At least, that's the way it will feel. We are all far more experienced and knowledgeable about narcissism these days and divorce courts have seen countless situations of this kind. That means you can be sure that everything will be fair in the eyes of those who are dealing with it from a legal point of view. However, don't expect fair from your partner.

It's probably against the rule we mentioned in our last chapter about being positive to say this, but you need to think of the worst case scenario here and try and prepare for it. By doing that, you're not going to be shocked or momentarily dumbfounded by what your narcissist says or does. Obviously, we hope that the worst case scenario you create in your mind doesn't come to fruition, but if it does, you'll be prepared.

Remember, divorcing a narcissist is a serious kick in the teeth to them, so you cannot expect anything positive from them.

Planning Your Finances and Housing

If you share finances at this point, you need to make sure that you have cash to be independent at the start. Your narcissist could quite possibly cut off access to joint accounts and whilst we don't know for sure that this will happen, it's something to be prepared for.

Ahead of time, start putting money aside for the period of time before the divorce is finalized and settled. If you're working and you have your own money, make sure your partner doesn't have access to it. This is even more important if you have children who rely upon your for care.

You should also look into possible benefits you can apply for if you're going to be struggling financially in the meantime. There are many places you can go to for help and advice and here you'll be able to find out if you're eligible for any financial help and how to apply for it. Find all of this information out before you leave, so you know what you're dealing with and you don't have any unnecessary shocks or surprises.

Of course, it's likely that as a married couple you're sharing a house. If you own the house between you, e.g. you have a mortgage then when the divorce is all finalized the house will make up part of the items and assets which are divided between you, however for now that needs to be put to one side.

Where are you going to live? You might think that you should be the one to stay in the marital home, especially if you have children, but your partner is likely to disagree. Remember, narcissists don't possess empathy or care for other people, so they're very unlikely to look at a situation through sensible eyes and come to the right choice. This is even more true if you decide to divorce them, as they're going to do everything they can to rebel against your decision and make life hard for you. That could include refusing to leave the marital home.

Whether you deem it right or not, it's best for you to be the one doing the leaving, at least for now. So, where will you go? Is there somewhere you can go and stay with a friend or a family member? Can you look to rent a house or an apartment in the meantime? Again, come up with a housing plan before you inform your partner of your decision, so you know what your immediate future is going to look like.

Do not make a move forwards with this divorce until you know what the road ahead looks like for the next six months or so. This is even more important if you have children, who need as much support and stability during this difficult time as possible.

DO YOU HAVE CHILDREN?

Let's focus on the idea of couples with children for a minute. If you don't have children, you can skip this section, but it might be useful to read it just so you can understand some of the lengths a narcissist will go to when riled or when they suffer what they assume to be a slight on their character.

If you have children you need to tread very carefully indeed, but that doesn't mean you shouldn't go ahead with your plans. If anything, it means you should be more determined in your choice.

We've already explained the fact that a narcissistic relationship is not healthy for children to be around. That's because children copy what their parents do; they learn by the example they're shown, so if they see their father or their mother treating their other parent in a way which isn't right, they're not going to realize that, they're going to think it is right and copy it. As a result, they grow up to repeat the habits that their narcissistic parent had. Or, they may go the other way and repeat the habits of the non-narcissistic parent, i.e. put up with treatment that they never deserved. Either way isn't positive or healthy for them.

Once you move forward with divorce proceedings and you have children, it's very likely that the narcissist is going to challenge you in court for custody of those children. They will do this because a) it's their child/children too, and b) they don't like to lose at anything.

Do not underestimate the lengths to which a narcissist will go in a divorce court. They will try and convince those making the decisions and helping you to come to fair arrangements that you're the bad parent. They will try and convince them that they're the one who can provide for your child best. They will try and make you look like you're emotionally unequipped, unbalanced, and not a competent parent. It will hurt, it will make you angry, but it's all the more reason to stick with the process.

We're going to talk about this a little later in the book but for all the reasons above, it's best to look into hiring a divorce lawyer who has experience of dealing with narcissistic divorce. They will help you side step these problems and hopefully come to the best conclusion for you and your family.

However, do not let the above put you off. You have to know what to expect so you can be prepared, but you should also know that positivity and the right decision will always shine through in the end. The narcissist might come over as a shining example of a parent, but they alone cannot make you look the opposite. Also, divorce professionals are very used to these types of tactics and are well-versed on what to look for.

Stand strong and remember that provided you're prepared and positive, nothing can shake you. Of course, that doesn't mean you should be seeking an unfair custody arrangement for your children either.

We can't give much of a comment on this particular issue, because we're not in your situation and we don't know the specifics, but overall, children need to spend time with both parents whenever it is pertinent or safe to do so. It's not a good idea to try and cut your child off from their other parent, simply because you're trying to get away from them and divorce the marriage. Remember, your child comes first.

We're not assuming that you would do this at all, but in some cases it's easy to try and do anything you can to get a narcissist out of your life. You will start off feeling sad about the whole divorce situation, but believe us, after you've been subjected to their very worst behavior throughout the proceedings, you're likely to change your mind and see that you're making the very best decision possible. In many ways, their negative behavior plays right into your hands.

However, always be fair and be the bigger person. When you do that, you'll always come away with a fair and acceptable arrangement for all involved, especially your children.

POINTS TO REMEMBER FROM THIS CHAPTER

This chapter is designed to help you put together a workable plan in the early stages of leaving your partner and seeking divorce. Doing some research in private, without telling your partner, means that you'll be prepared for the road ahead. That means putting a little money aside, making sure that you're financially covered, and maybe even making some appointments with benefits offices and finding out whether or not you'll be eligible for help if you happen to decide to go through with your plan.

You also need to think about housing, and maybe even start to rent a house or flat that you can move into immediately, and get away whilst the divorce proceedings run their course. Remember however, if there are children involved in the divorce, you need to do your very best to ensure that their life remains as normal as possible throughout it all.

The main points to take from this chapter are:

- You should think of the worst case scenario from your narcissist and go with that. When you opt for this route, you're not going to be surprised or shocked at anything they do and you're more likely to stand firm on your decision;

- Checking your options in terms of finances is a good idea before you tell anyone about your idea to divorce. This means you will have a comfort blanket of cash to keep you going throughout the process, especially if your partner decides to play unfair, which is possible;

- Look into benefits you might be able to apply for, in the event that you decide to leave your partner, especially if you have children;

- Do not assume that you will be able to stay in the marital home and that your partner will be the one to leave. Instead, look for somewhere else to stay in the meantime, until the dust settles. Again, do this all before you stay or do anything;

- If you have children you need to be prepared for the custody arrangements to be very difficult and probably quite upsetting. However, it's vital that you keep things as normal as possible for your child/children during the process.

CHAPTER 6:

DIVORCING A NARCISSIST

POINT 3 - INFORMING THE NARCISSIST

Once you're sure that you want to end your marriage to a narcissist, you need to think about the next step - informing them of your decision.

This can be a very difficult step to take, because of the nature of a narcissist in general.

To show you the difference, consider if you were going to tell someone without narcissistic traits that you wanted to divorce them. In most cases, you would be able to sit down and talk about the situation, explain your side, explore the problem and come to a mutual decision. Even if your partner wasn't in agreement completely or you didn't have the healthiest of relationships at that point, acceptance would come and you would be able to move through the process without too much drama.

However, when you're divorcing a narcissist, things can be very different.

A narcissist is likely to take the news that you want to not only leave, but divorce them, as extremely negative. They will see this as a serious slight on their character and an insult on them. They will twist everything around on you and they will aim to make you change your mind and apologize for even suggesting there is a problem.

It is at this stage you need to hold tightly to your reasons for wanting a divorce and not be wavered. If you allow yourself to move from your original decision at this point, life will not be easy moving forward. For starters, your partner will always remind you of what you almost did, throwing it in your face as though you did something to them. If you're sure, be firm and hold tight.

Informing the narcissist that you want a divorce is something you need to think about carefully beforehand, be sure of, and then do it, almost like pulling off a Band-Aid.

This chapter is designed to help you choose the right time and avoid the major pitfalls that may otherwise be associated with this vital step in the route towards freeing yourself of a narcissistic marriage.

CHOOSING THE RIGHT TIME

The first step is choosing the right time to tell the narcissist that you want to end the marriage. This isn't something you can do over dinner, and it's something you need to think about and plan carefully.

There are good times and bad times to have this conversation regardless of whether the relationship is touched by narcissism or not. For instance, if you were to tell your partner, narcissist or not, that you wanted a divorce, you wouldn't do it when they came home from work and seemed visibly irritated and stressed after a long day. Similarly, you wouldn't do it if they had just been given some bad news.

Choosing the right time is vital, but you should also be aware that this is not a discussion that is going to be smooth regardless of the time. You might think 'what's the point in choosing a good time if it's going to go bad anyway', but that's not the right mindset to have.

MAKING THE BEST OF A SITUATION IS VITAL IN THIS CASE.

Once you're sure you want a divorce, know what you're going to say. A little pre-planning will help you stay on target and ensure that you don't end up being swayed or saying the perceived 'wrong' thing. You can write it down and practice it beforehand if it gives you confidence, but you need to show the firmness and will to get away quite clearly to your narcissist.

If you show any amount of wobble or a perception that you may not be totally sure of your choice, your partner will pounce on that and use it against you. So, think about what you're going to say and practice saying it with confidence.

Then, when you're ready, gauge the right time. Choose a time when your partner seems relatively okay, i.e., not down or stressed and not having a 'moment' when they're likely to explode into a rage or a fit of passive-aggressive behavior. You might not understand your partner and their narcissism at times, but you know them best when it comes to the right time to deliver this kind of news.

Once you've identified a time which you think will work - go for it. Just do it.

If you think about it too much, you'll waver and you might never end up saying it. Then, time goes on and you change your mind. If you're sure, once the time presents itself, you have to just go for it.

Do's And Don'ts

So, what are the do's and don'ts of delivering this kind of news?

Firstly, remember that you're giving news that is likely to be taken badly and that is also likely to cause pain. Of course, narcissists don't feel things in the same way, but you have to respect the news you're giving enough to deliver it in a way that isn't insensitive. They might throw insensitive words at you on a regular basis, but you don't have to be the same; don't bow down to their level.

The exact do's and don'ts of this type of situation really depend upon the person involved. Again, you know your partner better than we do, but there are some general ideas that you can use when delivering this type of news.

Do's

- **Choose your time carefully** - We've just mentioned this, but it's worth placing it here and reinforcing the fact that timing is everything.

- **Know what you're going today and practice feeling confident with the words** - If you have a close friend you can speak to, practice with them. Having someone in front of you when you say words such as this can be much more powerful than saying it to yourself or in the mirror. Remember, you are admitting the fact that you want to end your marriage - this is something big and something which you can't just flippantly say in anger. It has to be done in the right way and using the right words.

- **Know that it's not going to be easy** - Your partner is not just going to shrug and say 'okay, I agree', they're not going to take it well. It could go a myriad of different ways, from silent treatment to rage, and everything else in-between, but you need to be aware of the fact that the discussion may be extremely difficult for you. This is where being strong and firm in your decision comes in.

- **Have a plan to leave the house afterward** - You don't know how your partner is going to react, and in that case having a plan to leave the house after giving the news is a good idea. Arrange to go and stay with a friend or family member for a few days, perhaps until things calm down and you feel a little stronger. Being in the same space as your partner after giving this news is not going to be a happy environment and it's likely to cause you to perhaps think back over your decision.

- **Be mindful of your body language** - When you're informing your partner of what you've decided, be mindful of what your body might be saying for you. Remember, you need to be confident and you need to be strong, even if inside you're not feeling that way at all. Hold eye contact, sit up straight, don't hold your arms across your body, and take deep breaths to control any nerves you're feeling. This will help you come over as more confident and sure and will stop the narcissist from pouncing on any perceived negative point.

- **Let them know that you've taken advice** - If you include a sentence that lets them know you've taken advice from a divorce lawyer, it strengthens your will and shows them that you're serious.

Don'ts

- **Allow yourself to be drawn into an argument** - It's very easy for a discussion such as this to turn into an argument, with accusations being thrown around. Instead, if your partner tries to make an argument, side step it and hold firm. It will take practice to be able to do this, but allowing the conversation to turn into an argument is not useful for anyone, and it's very unlikely that you will come out on top, such is the way of a narcissist.

- **Try and explain yourself further** - It's likely that your partner is going to try and get you to give examples of the behavior you're highlighting as a problem. This is done with the sole intention to make you doubt your choices, and it's not going to be productive for you. If your partner tries to push you and get you to keep explaining yourself, remember that this is a manipulation tactic that you do not need to indulge in. Simply say what you want to say and then end the conversation.

- **Let your buttons be pushed** - Your partner knows your sore spots and it's likely that they will try and use them at this point. Remember, to them, you wanting a divorce is the biggest insult. It won't be emotionally painful to them; it will be painful for their ego. As a result, they will try and deflect that pain onto you, and they know what buttons to press. Understand this and do not let yourself react as a result of them trying to poke away at your sore spots.

- **Expect anything positive** - We're not negative with this point, but it's important to think of the worst-case scenario here and then if it's a better scenario, that's good. Prepare yourself for a difficult conversation and then get out of there. If it goes well, then you can pat yourself on the back and be grateful for it, but expecting the worst will prepare you for anything your partner decides to throw at you.

WHAT TO EXPECT

We've given you some do's and don'ts of informing your narcissistic partner that you want a divorce and we've helped you find the right time to deliver the news. We've also told you that it's not going to be an easy discussion to have and you need to prepare yourself for anything, but what should you definitely expect?

Everyone is different, and you know your partner well. That means you'll have a better idea of what you might come up against when delivering very strong and serious news such as this. However, there are some very common narcissistic behavior traits that this type of situation will probably send your way.

If these don't happen in the midst of this type of discussion, then at least you were prepared for them.

So, what should you be prepared for?

As we've already mentioned, this type of news will come over to a narcissist as the worst type of slight. It will hurt them, but not in the same way it would hurt you. You would feel it emotionally, and your empathy would kick in, causing you to try and see things from your partner's side too. On the other hand, your partner doesn't have the empathy that you do, so they're not going to see your side of the issue, they're only going to see what it does to them.

They're going to blame you for hurting their ego and their self-esteem. They're going to think about how it's going to look to other people who might start to think of them in a lower way than the narcissists assumes they do now. They're going to be affronted that you dare even suggest they're anything less than the perfect husband or wife to you.

Of course, you know all of this to be false, but to the narcissist, it's completely clear. They will feel that you are the one causing the problem, you are the one making a huge drama, and you are the one hurting them above everything else. What they have done to you will not be called into question because, in their eyes, they've not even done anything. You are the one overreacting and it's all in your head.

Again, you know that's not true now, but your narcissist wants you to continue believing it to be the truth.

As we mentioned before, it's very likely that the narcissist will try and press your buttons at this point and even try and gaslight you, to get you to feel doubt and question your own decision. This is why you have to be sure and confident when telling them that you want a divorce. Even the slightest hint of doubt or nerves and they will pounce on it like a dog on a bone.

Again, expect the worst and perhaps hope for the best. It might be a negative mindset to have, but there's not a lot of positivity in this type of situation, when you know that the person you're trying to explain your feelings and decision to is not going to take in the way a normally functioning human being would. Remember, narcissists do not have emotions like yours, they do not feel empathy and they do not feel the love in the same way. So, how can you expect them to take news of a pending divorce in the same way?

You can't.

In many ways, you're in uncharted territory, but focusing on yourself is the best way through it. Keep remembering what you want your future to look like that you want to be free of feeling the way you do now. Do not let your partner sway your choices or your decisions based upon manipulation. You can see through it now and remember that it's all nothing but a sadistic game to them.

POINTS TO REMEMBER FROM THIS CHAPTER

In this chapter, we've talked about how and when you should deliver the news to your partner that you want a divorce. We've also mentioned several times that you should not expect this to be an easy or productive conversation. It's likely to be difficult and it's likely to be emotional. There may be times you start to question your choice, but you have to stand firm and know that your decision is final.

The main points to take from this chapter are:

- Informing your partner that you want a divorce is always a difficult conversation to have, but when your partner is a narcissist, you should expect a much more difficult ride;

- Your partner will not feel the news emotionally in the same way as you, because they are unable to feel empathy. Instead, they will take it as a slight on their character and their ego;

- You must find the right time to deliver the news;

- Practicing what you want to say beforehand will help you find the right words and be able to deliver them in a confident way;

- You should watch how your body language might be speaking for you at the same time as you actually verbalizing the words you want to say;

- You should prepare for the worst in terms of their reaction, and hope for the best.

CHAPTER 7:

DIVORCING A NARCISSIST

POINT 4 - HIRE SPECIALIST LEGAL HELP

A divorce is a legal procedure that ends a marriage in the eye of the law and therefore ensures that assets can be divided up fairly and equally between partners. If you have children, they will also help you to come to a custody arrangement, which is fair for both partners and above all else, fair for the child/ children.

However, in the situation that you find yourself in, it's important to look for specialist legal assistance if at all possible. This chapter is going to help you understand why specialist legal help, e.g., a divorce attorney who understands narcissistic behavior and the behavior and challenges that are likely to crop up during a divorce of this kind.

The Importance of Finding Out Information Beforehand

Before you say anything to your partner, make sure that you do your research and find out what you are entitled to. This is something we have already talked about, but it will give you confidence and also ensure that the route you have planned to be smoother than otherwise. If you simply jump in and expect everything to work out how you want it to, you might have a few surprises, and not particularly pleasant ones at that.

However, if you do your research and work out what you're entitled to, identify what you're going to do, and get all your plans organized, you'll find your route ahead will be far smoother as a result.

This also means doing your research into which particular professionals may be able to help you. Thankfully we have the Internet available to use 24/7 and this means you can find out useful and important information on anything you want to know, without really trying too hard.

A search of the local divorce attorneys in your area will give you plenty of options, but you can then narrow your search down by contacting the ones you think might be best for you and asking questions about anything you need to know. Many attorneys will offer you a consultation appointment and there may or may not be a fee for this. Again, this is something you need to find out beforehand.

The bottom line is that a divorce from a narcissist is a little different to a divorce from someone who doesn't have narcissistic tendencies. This is a divorce which has a very high likelihood of conflict, and one which may have twists and turns which probably wouldn't appear in what we could probably call a "regular" divorce. For that reason, you need to be confident in your future plan and have everything you want in front of you. This will help you to avoid going back on your decision, which is a very real possibility when a narcissist starts to turn on the charm, or even the abuse.

HOW A SPECIALIST DIVORCE ATTORNEY CAN HELP YOU

So, how can a divorce attorney who has specific experience in dealing with narcissists actually help you?

The bottom line is that they understand NPD, and that is a huge advantage in your court. They know that your partner is likely to try and say anything and as a result, they can be prepared for it and know how to deal with it. That's not to say an attorney who doesn't have experience of narcissism wouldn't be able to help you, but if you want the best chance of a successful outcome, and one which is less stressful and upsetting on you, a professional with this type of experience is a good idea.

This doesn't mean that this type of attorney has any other qualifications in the law field; it literally all comes down to experience and knowledge. It could be they have studied psychology or personality disorders as a separate line to their law-based work and that helps give them extra information about the situation you may find yourself in.

As we mentioned earlier, a divorce from a narcissist is also likely to be quite high in conflict, so looking for a divorce attorney who has experience in dealing with conflicts and resolving them in a fair and careful way is a plus point.

To summarize, the advantages of opting for a specialist divorce attorney are:

They understand NPD and therefore understand the challenges you face and the treatment you have been subjected to over the year

They have experience in dealing with conflicts and they have specific skills to help resolve high conflict situations

They know what to expect from NPD, so can possibly help to predict the challenges that might lie ahead

Of course, you also need to be sure that any divorce attorney you opt to work with is within your budget, and that means doing extra research. It's worthwhile going for what you really can afford in this situation, as your divorce attorney is the single best person to deal with this problem from the start, and therefore take the workload and the stress away from you. You have dealt with enough, and if you can reduce your own problems after the decision to walk away from your marriage, you should certainly do that.

BE HONEST ABOUT EVERYTHING AND WORK OUT YOUR CASE

Once you've found a divorce attorney who can help you and someone you feel comfortable with, it is vital that you tell them as much as you possibly can. The more open and honest you are, the more your attorney can help you. If you hold anything back, your partner might decide to twist that detail in court and as a result you're left in the dark, because your attorney isn't able to help you on the spot.

It's likely to be painful having to open up about the abuse you have dealt with at the hands of your ex and it's very normal to feel perhaps even a little embarrassed, but you have to push this aside. You have nothing to be ashamed of, nothing to be embarrassed about, and you really just need to open up and give your attorney as much information to work with as possible. By doing this, they will be able to prepare themselves for whatever your ex throws at you during the divorce proceedings. As we've already mentioned, you should expect the worst and hope for the best, and you can help your attorney prepare for the worst by giving them as much information as possible, whether you struggle to give graphic details about it all or not.

From there, sit down with your attorney and work out your case. What do you want? What are your hard lines? If you have children, what are you prepared to do in terms of custody arrangements? Thinking about assets, how do you want to split things and how are you going to work out what goes to who?

At this stage, you're not deciding; this will be decided in the divorce courts, but you can lay out your offer and as a result your attorney can get to work on making sure that you have a case which has the best chance of giving you what you really want in the end.

It can be difficult to sit down and tell a relative stranger about what you have endured at the hands of your partner over the years, but it's something you have to try and be brave about and just do. The more information you can give, the better prepared your attorney will be, and that greater the chances of a quick and successful outcome for you.

Points to Remember From This Chapter

When going through any divorce, you will need the help of an attorney to help negotiate assets and other items which need to be shared between the two of you. Your attorney is also there to ensure that you have a fair outcome to the divorce and that the filed reason for divorce isn't inaccurate on your side.

A divorce attorney is a specialist in family law, helping to focus on the breakdown of a relationship to the point where divorce is wished for, and if you have children, they can help to arrange your custody arrangements and child support. By having a highly qualified attorney in your corner, you have a much better chance of a fair and happy outcome.

It's a good idea to look into divorce attorneys who have experience of narcissism too, as this will boost your own case.

The main points to take from this chapter are:

- A divorce lawyer is a specialist in family law and can, therefore, help you to share assets, come to fair arrangements on custody and child support payments, and also help with the upheaval and general upset that comes alongside the divorce of a marriage;

- Some divorce lawyers have experience in dealing with NPD, and if you can find a specialist in this area, it's a good idea to go with them;

- A divorce lawyer with experience of dealing with NPD will be able to help you overcome the challenges that tend to work hand in hand with divorcing a narcissist, and will understand the very subtle yet strong differences which narcissists can bring to the divorce table;

- It's important to be as open and honest with your divorce lawyer as possible, to ensure that they have all the information they need to help you reach a fair outcome to your divorce.

Chapter 8:

Divorcing a Narcissist

Point 5 - Retain Any Evidence

By this point, you should be very clear of the difficult task in front of you, but you should also be very clear in your mind that it's not impossible and that thousands of people before you have done the exact same thing, perhaps even millions worldwide.

The divorce proceedings are likely to be very long, painful, and complicated, because a narcissist will never give in. They do not want anyone to see them as anything other than wonderful and they assume that by divorcing them, you're trying to paint them in a light that they don't believe they deserve. As a result, they will throw all kinds of mud at you and wait for it to stick. This is why having a divorce attorney who understands narcissism will serve you well. In this case, your attorney will know how to side steps that mud and help you duck any potential damage to both your reputation and your livelihood.

The divorce is likely to come down to your word against their kind of situation. This is typical and very normal for this type of situation. However, that makes it hard for you to believe that you're going to end up coming out of the divorce in a happier situation than you went into it. It can happen and it will happen, provided you can be as positive as possible and make sure you tick all the necessary boxes.

One of those boxes is ensuring that you retain copies of any useful evidence.

Remember, when it comes down to a situation, which is basically your word against theirs, it's useful to have something to back your side up and therefore discredit what your partner is saying. This will cast a huge amount of confusion over any of their arguments from that point onwards and could swing the whole thing firmly in your favor.

NARCISSISTS ARE EXCELLENT LIARS

You might wonder why you need to go around collecting evidence as though you're in an episode of CSI, but the fact remains that narcissists are extremely good at lying. Even when a narcissist is lying, they believe they're telling the truth. This helps them come across as completely truthful, because they don't display the same tell-tale body language signs as someone who is lying and knows they are.

For instance, if you're lying, you probably avoid looking someone in the eye, because deep down, you feel quite guilty about the tale you're telling. You might fidget, and you might even sweat. When a narcissist is lying, they don't show any of these signs, because they believe in the lie they're telling. They don't believe they have to defend themselves because there is nothing to defend in their own minds.

This can make it very difficult for you in a divorce court, if necessary, because they're so convincing. This is why having evidence of anything you're using as part of your divorce case is vital.

Lies sit right at the heart of narcissism. Remember, this is someone who is creating an illusion of wonderment, because they feel so low in confidence deep down. In order to pull this off, they have to 100% believe the pretense they're setting. A narcissist does not go to bed at night and feel bad or guilty about anything they've said or done, and they don't worry about being found out. Why would they when they don't believe there is anything to be found out in the first place?

WHAT COUNTS AS 'EVIDENCE'?

What exactly can you use as evidence?

It's a good idea to keep hold of any papers you have, particularly anything related to expenses and financial situations. If there is paper-based evidence there, the lies of a narcissist are completely blown apart.

You should also keep hold of any texts or emails you have received, especially if someone you say is thrown back at you by your ex and the whole he said/she said situation rears its head. This is quite easy to do these days, especially if you use a messaging app such as WhatsApp or Facebook Messenger. This app holds your entire conversation in one thread, so you can simply scroll and screenshot the message you want and show it as necessary. Emails do need to retained however, so make sure that you're mindful of this at the time.

Financial evidence is quite easy to hold these days too, as Internet banking will give a rolling statement of your cash flowing into and out of your account. Make sure you keep up with access on any joint accounts and before you even tell your partner that you are filing for divorce, obtain print outs of the statement. This means that if your partner attempts to close the account or make any changes to it, you have the evidence you need already in your pocket.

POINTS TO REMEMBER FROM THIS CHAPTER

The idea of keeping evidence against your partner might be quite upsetting for you but you have to remember that the lies that are likely to be thrown at you aren't coming from a place of love either. A narcissist lies without even thinking about it, and they don't understand the concept of guilt or shame.

As a result, you're likely to find yourself in a your word against theirs kind of situation. A way through this is to keep as much paper-based evidence as possible, including messages, emails, texts, and if possible, financial records and expenditure.

The main points to take from this chapter are:

- Narcissist are born liars and the lies they tell don't register on their radar as untrue, they firmly believe them
- It is very likely to come down a situation in a divorce court where it's your word against theirs. In that case, any evidence you can show is vital
- Keep hold of messages, texts and emails to show as evidence, and any financial or expenditure records if possible.

CHAPTER 9:
DIVORCING A NARCISSIST
POINT 6 - DO NOT CHANGE YOUR MIND

We're covering a lot of information that you need to know when divorcing a narcissist specifically, but at this halfway point of the process, there is one thing you need to remember and remind yourself of - never change your mind.

Your ex is very likely to throw everything at you during the divorce proceedings and at the point when you inform them of what you want, but it's vital that you hold firm. We've mentioned this a few times already, but as you move through the process, there is likely to be a nagging doubt enter your mind at some stage.

Do not listen to it.

If you change your mind and call off the divorce at this point, your partner is going to make your life a literal living hell. They will not take anything you say seriously at that point, if they ever did before, they will never let you forget the perceived injustice that you attempted to impart on them and there is very unlikely to be any joyful times from that point onwards.

REMEMBER YOUR PRIMARY MOTIVATION

Remember the reason you wanted the divorce in the first place. What was it that triggered you and made you make that decision? What was the lightbulb moment?

Remember it, pull it to the front of your mind and commit it to your memory. Write it down and look at it regularly if you need to, but this is something you must remember at all times. Your primary motivation for leaving is the point that tipped you over the edge and make you suddenly realize that you deserve better. That is a positive moment for you, something which urged you to take action and leave a situation which caused you nothing but pain and confusion, even if you didn't realize it wasn't your fault at the time.

When things get tough when your partner starts to throw everything including the kitchen sink your way, when they try and convince everyone that you're lying and they're perfect, visualize that moment you made the decision that you wanted a divorce. Remember how it felt when you suddenly realized that you don't have to deal with this anymore.

Some people find it useful to meditate and try and pull the exact moment to their minds. Visualization is a very powerful tool and it can help you to remember the reasons why you made your decision. That reason hasn't changed and hasn't gone away; it's simply buried underneath a lot of confusion and pain, the normal situation that occurs in the middle of a divorce. The only difference with a divorce from a narcissistic that you're likely to feel even more confused, because the gaslighting doesn't end.

TURNING ON THE CHARM

There are two main ways in which a narcissist will deal with the divorce, so let's look at those in turn now.

Firstly, they might turn on the charm. If they don't do this fully, they will use this tactic periodically throughout the divorce process. This is designed to make you remember the good times and therefore think twice about continuing with the divorce.

They will suddenly go back to the person they were when you first met, when everything was wonderful and you felt like you had met the most amazing person in the world. Remember, they are not that person in reality, they are acting and everything they are showing you is nothing but an act.

It is a form of emotional abuse because the sole aim is to make you fall in love all over again and not want to end the connection you have. The problem is, once they see that you've chosen to stay in the relationship and not go through with the divorce, they're going to go back to the way they were before, if not worse. Probably worse.

ABUSE COMING YOUR WAY

The other possibility is that a constant stream of abuse is going to come your way instead. This could actually work hand in hand with the charm, but at some point, the abuse will give way and you'll be subjected to constant lies, passive-aggressive behavior, insults, and basically making you look like the bad guy.

In some ways, whilst the abuse is terrible and upsetting, it's less likely to make you want to go back to your partner! Having said that, it could be extremely damaging your self-esteem and make you think about things which have happened in the past. The gaslighting which narcissists are known for could also cause to believe that certain events were your fault, when they most certainly were not.

It's vital that you're prepared for both sides of the coin, but also that you remember your reason for wanting a divorce in the first place, and keep that in your mind when you might start to waver and wonder whether this entire process is what you really want.

If you hadn't wanted it completely, you wouldn't have made the decision. Any thoughts on changing your mind are firmly down to the way your ex is handling the situation themselves and their behavior towards you. Take them out of the equation from this point onwards and focus entirely on yourself instead. That is the best way to deal with it all.

However, you should recognize that having second thoughts during any divorce is normal, but it doesn't mean you should change your mind. You shared feelings at some stage and you were in love, enough to marry them in the first place. Of course, it's going to be hard and you're going to wonder whether you're doing the right thing, but when it comes to getting away from a narcissistic relationship, you're always doing the right thing.

Always.

Points to Remember From This Chapter

This chapter has been a bit of a pep talk and is designed to make you realize that at some stage during the divorce, you're probably going to wonder whether you're making the right decision in going through with it.

This could be down to a charm offensive, albeit a fake one, or it could be because your ex is continuing to gaslight you and make you feel like everything is your fault. Either way, you have to stand firm and remember the reason why you wanted a divorce in the first place.

Nobody said it would be easy, but it will certainly be worth it.

The main points to take from this chapter are:

- It's normal to wonder whether you're doing the right thing at some stage during a divorce;

- You need to remember your primary motivation for asking for a divorce in the first place;

- A narcissist is likely to take the fact you have asked for a divorce extremely personally and will, therefore, react in a way which pulls you down, rather than builds you up;

- You may be subjected to an onslaught of charm, designed to make you remember the good times when you first got together;

- You will certainly be subjected to abuse at some stage during the divorce, designed to make you look bad and your partner looks good.

CHAPTER 10:
DIVORCING A NARCISSIST
POINT 7 - PLANNING THE DIVIDING OF ASSETS

In a "regular" divorce, assets are split fairly and equally between both partners, however, when you are divorcing a narcissist, you should not expect the division of assets to run as smoothly as it may otherwise do.

Remember, everything is a game and a competition to a narcissist. In their eyes, they want to receive more from this division of assets because that shows they are better than you. They do not see this in the same way as you, or in the same way as most other people, if we're frankly honest.

A narcissist has to be seen as better than everyone around them and that means that 'equal' doesn't fall into their remit or their vocabulary. If you're expecting assets to be divided down the middle and split fairly, you're going to be shocked at the lengths your partner may go to, simply to try and get a little more than you do.

For this reason, opting for specialist legal representation in the form a divorce attorney who has experience in dealing with narcissists, is vital.

THINK BEFORE YOU ACT

We're going to reiterate this same point once more, because it is so vital, especially at this stage. You need to know what you want and need beforehand, so your divorce attorney can put their own case forward and plans in place to ensure you get it. This means understanding your financial situation, what you need in order to survive financially after the divorce is granted, and knowing that you aren't going to come out of the divorce financially worse off than you were before.

This all comes down to careful and proper planning and is also something which your divorce attorney can help you with.

Due to the rather unpleasant and sometimes unforthcoming attitude of a narcissist, it may be that you need to communicate in this part of the divorce in a written manner. Again, this is something you can discuss and work out with your attorney. This helps to limit the anguish and upset, which may be caused, trying to communicate directly with your partner. Remember, narcissists aren't the greatest at telling the truth and when the sole reason for being a part of these negotiations is simply to make you look back, they are likely to go all out to make that happen.

It's very likely that your partner will not be particularly forthcoming when it comes to financial information. In our last chapter, we mentioned keeping evidence of everything when it comes to property division, that is extremely important. The divorce process will stall and become very long-winded if you allow the narcissist to control proceedings, because they want to do everything on their terms. A narcissist is not going to repent anything and they're not going to say "oh okay, you have that".

If you opt to deal with your partner via written communication rather than verbal, you are able to think before you speak and put together a case which is far stronger as a result. The narcissist's power is diminished when this happens and your power is stronger.

If your partner controlled your finances before the divorce decision, again, be sure to get copies of statements and other papers before you tell them you're opting for a divorce. By doing that, you'll ensure that the asset and property division side of the procedure runs a little smoother than it otherwise might.

The IRS is able to help you obtain information on your tax issues and you may also be able to get extra financial information by running a simple credit check. These are also things you can do prior to the divorce, and have the information to hand, to give to your divorce attorney.

Housing Issues

Whilst you probably love your marital home, you have to ask yourself whether you want to live in it, with all the memories, after the divorce. This is something you need to think about and it really comes down to who owns the house or whether you're renting.

If you are both homeowners, i.e., you have a joint mortgage, you will need to go through the courts to decide who gets what, etc. If, however, you're renting, it may simply be the best idea to cut your losses and move to another house, which doesn't have the haunting memories of the last one. It's not worth going through a housing battle with your ex for a rented property; they will make it extremely hard for you and they're not going to concede an inch. Why go through this for a house that isn't yours in the first place?

If however you own the house, you have a few things to think about.

What do you want to do about it?

Do you want to fight for the house? Do you want to cut your losses and accept payment for your half? Think about it carefully and work out your final option. You can then communicate your desires to your divorce attorney and they can work hard to try and get you what you want.

Do however remember that although your narcissistic ex is not being fair to you, by law they are still entitled to half of everything (in theory), so you have to ensure that your demands and needs are fair too.

Be the bigger person and be the fair person. If they want to go all out to muddy your name and try and make life difficult, let them; in the end, the right side of things always shines through. However, the housing issue side of a divorce is often the most contentious for couples who don't have children. If you have children, that's always going to be the most difficult side of the story.

In terms of a completely fresh start, consider whether you want to live in the house or not.

CUSTODY PROBLEMS

If you have children, the care of your dependents will obviously be at the forefront of your mind. As with everything else related to divorcing a narcissist, your ex is not going to make this side of things easy for you. Again, this is why you need a specialist divorce attorney.

It's not unusual for a narcissist to throw an extreme amount of shade at their ex and try and make them look like an unfit parent, when the complete opposite is true. The hardest thing in the world is trying to remain passive and let things go over your head, but in this situation, you have to try your best.

You should not allow your child to become a pawn in the middle of your divorce and that means ensuring that whatever arrangement you come to in terms of custody, is fair at all costs. This is the thing you should fight hardest for.

Again, keep copies of everything, including messages and emails that might show the divorce courts the extent of the narcissistic abuse you may have been subjected to. This will always indirectly affect your child, so showing this information will help them to access a brighter future out of the divorce also.

Again, be prepared for anything, but also remember that your ex is also your child's parent and that they also deserve to have a relationship with their child. Once more, you need to be the bigger person, and as difficult as that can be, you need to show that you're able to see the best for your child, no matter what.

The options available to you are sole custody, joint custody, visitation rights, third party custody. You know what is best for your child, so this isn't something we can advise you on right now, but again, explore your options and know the ins and outs of all routes forward. By doing this, you can come to a suitable arrangement for the both of you.

Despite that, don't expect your narcissistic ex to make it easy for you.

Whilst some custody arrangements can be made out of court and quite easily, it's very unlikely to be the case for you. A narcissistic isn't likely to give up anything, let alone custody of their child. In that case, you're probably going to end up with your case in a family law court, with a mediator working between you. Preparing for that reality is something you must do to ensure you're not shocked or surprised when a difficult road ahead presents itself.

When deciding upon the best custody arrangement for a child, the court will take into account the current living situation, e.g., where you live versus where the child goes to school. They will also ask the child their preference, if they're old enough, as well as any evidence which may point towards the suitability of one parent over another. If a child is young enough, e.g., a baby or toddler still being breastfed, the court may also place preference toward the mother, for the reason of basic care.

If there is sufficient evidence of abuse towards the child, this will go against the parent it pertains to. However, if there is zero evidence of abuse towards the child, but you can prove that you were subjected to emotional abuse at the hands of your narcissistic partner, you may find yourself in a grey area. Again, this is where you need to show evidence and hard proof of what you were subjected to, so the courts can decide whether this is likely to have affected the child, or whether it will do at any point in the future.

Of course, the issue of child support will also need to be discussed. We would like to think that your ex will be more than happy to pay their fair share of expenses when it comes to looking after your child, but we cannot predict the actions of a narcissist. Again, if they're hell-bent on making you look like the guilty partner and painting themselves as a victim, they may be overly generous, or they may refuse completely. In that case, the courts will decide how much and how often child support will need to be paid, and by whom.

GENERAL DIVORCE DIVISION OF ASSETS

Whilst you might think that division of assets will always be 50/50, this isn't always the case. The court can decide to grant a greater amount towards one partner than the other, depending upon the situation at hand.

We can only speak in general terms here as we don't have information on your specific situation and financial circumstances, but the general division of assets in a divorce center around the following:

- Any real estate holdings
- Any income which has been received on non-marital home property
- Retirement and pension funds
- Stocks and shares, and any other investments
- Any deferred income
- Any business owned by the family and the valuation estimate
- Inheritance or heirlooms
- Any collectible items
- Cars or other vehicles
- Boats
- Hidden assets

You may have information to hand on these, if they pertain to you, but again, it pays to seek out information beforehand, to ensure that your partner doesn't attempt to withhold information or make the division of assets harder and more laborious than it needs to be.

POINTS TO REMEMBER FROM THIS CHAPTER

This chapter has been about the division of assets within a divorce, while also touching upon the subject of child custody and child support payments. You might think it rather crass to mention custody of a child within a chapter on asset division, but we simply wanted you to have a full overview of the negotiations which may take place within the divorce proceedings, depending upon your situation.

For sure, if you don't have children, then your divorce will be a little easier than if you do have children. That's not to say it's going to be plain sailing by any means, but not having to negotiate custody and child support does take a weight off. However, if you do have children, ensuring that you work towards a fair and happy solution for your child is vital. Opting for a specialized divorce attorney will allow you to do this, whilst also understanding the particular challenge and perils which lie ahead, when divorcing a narcissistic partner.

The main points to take from this chapter are:

- Divorce proceedings divide up assets between partners on a fair and equal basis;

- The division isn't always a strict 50/50 split and in some cases, the courts can decide to grant one partner a greater share, depending upon the situation at hand;

- You need to decide beforehand what you want and what is important to you, and then communicate this information to your divorce attorney. They can then work their case around this and do their best to ensure that you get what you need from the final arrangement;

- If you own your home with your partner, you need to think very carefully about what you want to happen to the property. Do you want to stay, or do you want to be free of the memories? If you rent, it's probably a better idea to cut your losses and move to another property;

- Ensuring the right child custody arrangement is the most important aspect of the proceedings, if you have children. However, it's likely that your custody arrangements will be finalized in court, and not in a fair way between the two of you;

- It is a good idea to obtain copies of any financial documents before you tell your partner that you're opting for a divorce. A narcissist is not likely to be that open about the financial side of things, as they rate material items and money over feelings and fairness.

Chapter 11:
Divorcing a Narcissist
Point 8 - Ensure You Have Support at Every Step

Divorces are hard, whether they involve a narcissistic partner or not. The easiest divorce on the planet is still hard on the emotions and involves a lot of looking back and wondering what went wrong. That doesn't even take into account the uncertainty, the financial side of things, and the attempt to move forward with your life, without the so-called 'safety net' that your narcissistic partner provided during your time together.

It's not unusual for partners of narcissists to feel extremely alone and unable to cope after walking away. A narcissist is the ultimate control freak, and that means they're likely to have taken control of everything, meaning that you might need to learn a few new tricks in order to take back control of your life.

For instance, did your partner deal with all the finances? In that case, you need to learn how to open a bank account, traverse your way around Internet banking, learn about the bills you need to pay every month, change names of accounts, etc. This can be a little daunting if you've never done it before, especially when you're trying to build up your confidence and your sense of self-worth after coming out of a relationship that has been so emotionally abusive.

For this reason, you need to make sure that you have support throughout every step of the divorce proceedings and at the point when you decide to leave your partner in the first place. Sure, you have your divorce attorney at your side and they will certainly provide you with a huge amount of support, but in terms of the emotional side of things, you can't beat a close friend or family member being there for you when you need them.

HAVE YOU BEEN ISOLATED?

The biggest problem for most people who break away from narcissistic relationships is that throughout their time with their partner, they probably became quite isolated.

This is a classic manipulation tactic by a narcissistic, who will usually try and move their partner away from their closest friends and family. They do this because deep down, they're quite terrified that those around them will see that they're not all that authentic and will try and warn their friend or family member away. They're worried you will listen, so they do everything they can to isolate you and make you completely dependent upon them for your social and supportive needs. Of course, they don't support you at all, and certainly not in the way you need it.

They're likely to do this by telling you that someone has been talking behind your back, e.g., your best friend was heard telling people that you're stupid, etc. This is done in order to manipulate you away. Of course, your friend didn't say those things, but they'll do everything they can to make you think that way. By doing this, you're forced to choose between your partner and your closest friends; the terrible thing is that you're more likely to choose your partner, such is the amount of reliability you've developed upon them.

The good news is that if your family and friends are genuine, they're going to be relieved when you reach out, but you need to find the strength to simply say "please help me, I need you". It's the strongest thing you will ever do and it's certainly not a weakness in any way to be able to say you need a little support to make it through a difficult time.

CREATING YOUR SUPPORT CIRCLE

In order to create a rock-solid support circle, you need to be open and honest with whoever you choose to reach out to. Don't be afraid to admit what has happened, how you've felt, what you've been through, etc. The more you open up, the more they can help you overcome your experiences and gain strength for the next chapter.

We've already mentioned that your divorce attorney will be able to help support you throughout proceedings, but in terms of close support, in terms of being there when you might be experiencing a flashback, worrying about something, or generally feeling terrible about everything that's happened, a close friend or family member is best.

There are also many support groups to be found online or even in your local area perhaps who can help you to come to terms with not only the end of a marriage, which his sad enough in itself, but also the narcissistic abuse you have been subjected to over the period of time before.

As before, be open and honest about what has happened and don't be scared of being vulnerable.

The more you open up, the more people will be able to help you, support you, and allow you to gain straight throughout the divorce proceedings and beyond.

When should you gather your support circle? The moment you realize that you need to do so. When you decide that you're going to walk away from the marriage and divorce your partner, look towards those around you for support. This decision in itself is tough, but when you add the abuse side of things into the equation, it can be ten times harder.

Don't be afraid to seek help from those you may have pushed away in the past - they're waiting for you to draw them close again.

HEALING PAST WOUNDS

In some cases, gaining the support you need might require you to heal a few wounds.

Don't be afraid of doing this, and once you've explained the situation to them, they will understand why everything happened the way it did.

This might be the case if someone close to you was pushed away and they still don't quite understand why or what happened. Call a meeting, talk, be honest, be open, apologize if you need to and help them to understand why you went MIA and pushed them away. This is all part of your recovery process and once you solve this problem, you can look forward to a future which is full of those close to you. Of course, this also helps you in the current moment because this person is then able to be there for you and help you through the next few months ahead.

POINTS TO REMEMBER FROM THIS CHAPTER

This chapter's aim is to help you understand that you cannot and should not do this alone. You may have pushed people away or become isolated during your time with your partner, but opening up to these people, being honest and open, and explaining the situation will set you free.

The main points to take from this chapter are:

- You will need a support network around you, to help you get through the divorce and beyond;

- Your divorce attorney is part of your support network, but you need emotional support too, the kind which can often only be provided by close family and friends;

- It's possible that you need to apologize and help those around you understand what happened - don't be afraid to do this;

- Reaching out to people and asking for help isn't a weakness; it's a true strength.

CHAPTER 12:

DIVORCING A NARCISSIST

POINT 9 - ALLOW YOURSELF THE TIME TO HEAL

Once the divorce is over, or it is nearing the end, you need to give yourself time to grieve.

Every divorce is hard and every divorce is the end of an era. Whether your partner was a narcissist or not, you are ending a relationship with someone you loved, and perhaps on some level someone you still love to this day. The fact you have realized that you deserve better, that you deserve someone who will love you the way you are, without the need for manipulation means that you've chosen to put yourself first.

Of course, this also means that you need to avoid jumping into another relationship straight away and give yourself the time to heal from the abuse you've been subjected to.

Many victims of narcissistic abuse require professional help after the event, in order to help them make sense of the experience, to separate themselves from what really went on, to help them see that none of it was actually their fault, and then to start looking towards the future with a sense of positivity, building up their confidence with time.

You should not expect miracles overnight. Every single divorce, touched by narcissism or not, is a life milestone which is hard to handle. Just because you're escaping from a difficult situation doesn't make the fact you're ending a marriage any easier to deal with.

We've talked about the main points to remember when it comes to divorcing a narcissist and this final chapter is designed to wrap everything up and summarize to the final parting point. It's also designed to help you understand that when you receive the notification that your divorce is final, that doesn't mean that you're suddenly going to have washed your hands of everything you dealt with, you've made peace with it, and suddenly everything feels normal again. It may take time, and in some cases, considerable time, to feel like everything is back on track. It can also take time for you to finally understand for sure that none of it was your fault. In many ways, you need to forgive yourself in order to move on.

THE EFFECTS OF NARCISSISTIC ABUSE

Depending upon how bad the abuse was, you're likely to suffer from a few after-effects. You will certainly be quite mistrusting for a while and when you look back at what you've been through, it's hardly surprising. However, it's important to remember that not everyone is the same as your ex, and that people who treat you in this way are actually in the minority.

It's also vital to remember that you're not the same as anyone else either, and just because one person who has suffered from narcissistic abuse reacted in one way, doesn't mean you're going to follow suit. However you feel, whatever you go through, it's normal for you and that's an important point to remember.

If you think back to our first chapter, when we talked about what narcissism actually is, you'll remember that the main aim of a narcissist is to make their partner;

- Question their own mind and sanity
- Question and become distrustful of their closest family and friends

- Feel as though the only person who cares about them is their narcissistic partner, resulting in extremely low self-worth
- Feel unable to make decisions or think for themselves
- Become completely disconnected from anything they want, need, or dream about and become completely about serving the narcissist instead
- Become obsessive about every mistake or problem in their lives
- Overlook everything the narcissist does and make excuses for them
- Put the narcissist on a pedestal and do everything to make them happy

When you break it down like that, you can see just how abusive and controlling a narcissistic relationship is. You have paid yourself no credit or care for so long that you've forgotten what it feels like to be loved and cared about genuinely. That even means you've forgotten how to love yourself.

With that in mind, the road back can be lengthy and it's likely to take time and effort to get back to feeling like yourself. It's also likely that you'll feel changed forever, as though a part of your is tainted by the narcissistic abuse and no longer able to see things with hope. With time that will eventually change too, and you'll start to open your eyes to the wonder of the world.

Many victims of narcissistic abuse come out of the relationship, whether married or not, feeling completely worthless. It's possible to have flashbacks, panic attacks, to doubt yourself completely and worry about making decisions, and you might feel like you've lost your support crutch, now that the narcissist is no longer in your midst.

Narcissistic abuse syndrome is a very real thing. This is the after-effects of a narcissistic relationship, or the effects that are happening during the relationship, with a victim reaches out for help and support. The victim is often so low in confidence and self-worth that they're completely ravaged emotionally.

Of course, you might not be at this end of the spectrum, or you might be, the point remains that you will have some scar of the relationship and you need to give yourself the adequate amount of time to heal and move on.

Many healthcare professionals compare narcissistic abuse to post-traumatic stress disorder. The after-effects can come in the form of the flashbacks we mentioned earlier, panic attacks, and problems trusting other people. From that, you can see just how seriously a person can be affected by narcissism, and that by breaking free, you've only really taken the first step, albeit a very important one, towards recovery.

SEEKING PROFESSIONAL HELP

Many victims of narcissistic abuse end up seeking professional help, and if you feel that you need it, you should certainly go for it. You don't need to do this alone, and it might be that your friends and family give you enough support, but still don't quite get to the heart of the issue.

Healthcare professionals are seeing more and more people visiting their clinics and centers who are suffering the after-effects of narcissistic abuse. There are groups set up to help support people like you, and there are countless other men and women out there who can sit down with you and have a conversation that is so deep and completely on your level, because they 100% understand exactly what you've been through - all because they've been through it too.

Sometimes that's all you need, someone to be able to relate from the personal experience completely. Of course, it might be that you need something a little more in-depth, and if that's the case, again, take it.

Counseling, therapy, medical interventions, these are all available for victims of narcissistic abuse and talking to your doctor, or a healthcare professional in general will allow you to access these help methods and look forward to a brighter future.

Post traumatic stress disorder (PTSD) is a form of mental health condition. Someone who has come out of a narcissistic relationship and is so badly shaken to the core by the manipulation and mental and emotional abuse they've been subjected to falls into this category. That doesn't mean you're failing, it means you've been through something hard and you need help.

Many divorcees suffer from depression and anxiety at the end of a marriage, even a marriage which isn't connected to narcissism in any way. It's like a death in some ways; you're grieving the end of something which you thought would last forever, and the realization that it's not going to be can be very hard to deal with. When you add manipulation and abuse onto that, you can understand that the picture can be extremely dark and distressing.

You do not have to go through your life struggling for a second longer; the help is out there, you simply need to ask for it.

DON'T RUSH INTO A NEW LIFE

Part of the recovery after any divorce is to give yourself time to heal and recover, but after a narcissistic relationship, that is even more important. You cannot and should not attempt to jump into another relationship simply because you think that's going to block out the memory of the one before.

If you do that, you're simply carrying old baggage into a new relationship and not allowing yourself the time to process what happened and understand the fact that it wasn't your fault. You're more likely to repeat the same patterns of behavior as a result, which will put pressure on your new relationship, making it more likely to fail.

You will not be able to have a happy and healthy relationship until you have processed the events of your former marriage and made peace with it. After that, of course, you have every chance of falling in love once more, but that doesn't mean you have to either. If you want to continue your life and enjoy time alone, that's perfectly fine too. Go with whatever feels good for you.

Another point to be aware of is to avoid jumping into unhealthy habits as a way to mask what you're feeling. Firstly, distraction techniques are never a good idea, because you're basically masking the problem and not dealing with it, and secondly, if you opt for an unhealthy coping choice, such as smoking, drinking, eating too much, shopping, etc., then you're causing yourself another problem on top of the heartache and pain that you're trying to heal from.

For your own good, make sure that you focus on healthy routes forward and learn to handle the pain and the upset that you've been through. There are plenty of people out there who are waiting and willing to help you and to access that help, you simply need to reach out and ask.

WHAT DOES THE FUTURE HOLD?

Life after a divorce can be strange for a while. You had your life mapped out, you thought you knew who you were going to spend the rest of your days with, but suddenly everything changes and you're left wondering what you're supposed to do.

This feeling is normal and it's something you have to face in order to move on. The world is full of exciting opportunities and these will come to you over the days, weeks, months, and years to come. You will not be able to see them and grasp them in all their positive glory unless you do what we've tried to explain to you throughout this chapter - understand and deal with what's happened before jumping into a new life.

Your future does not have to be the same as your past. You have made a huge leap of faith by leaving your marriage to a narcissist and going through the very tough, yet necessary, divorce proceedings. Now, you're free to live your life and understand that you're a wonderful, worthwhile person who doesn't deserve to be controlled by anyone.

POINTS TO REMEMBER FROM THIS CHAPTER

This final chapter has been somewhat of a pep talk. Hopefully, you'll be feeling a little more upbeat and positive about your future at this point. You've been through a lot, and if you're still to go through the divorce proceedings, you'll know that you have a lot more in front of you. You will survive it however, because you're armed with the knowledge that you needed. If you surround yourself with your support network and keep a brighter future at the front of your mind, you'll get through it and free yourself completely.

Despite all of this you need to understand that it won't be easy and you're sure to experience a few after-effects. If you need help, if you really feel like you're struggling, embrace that and ask for support. It's completely normal to experience effects after escaping from a narcissistic relationship. PTSD (post-traumatic stress disorder) is also linked to victims of narcissistic abuse, so if you really feel you need help, get it. If you're not sure if you need help, get it anyway. You can never be too sure, and your future is too precious to play Russian roulette with.

The main points to take from this chapter are:

- Narcissistic abuse leaves scars and you may need professional help after leaving your partner in order to cope and move on;

- Divorce of any kind can leave you feeling low, possibly even depressed and anxious - you do not have to face this alone;

- Many victims of narcissistic abuse display symptoms of post-traumatic stress disorder, such as panic attacks and flashbacks;

- It's important not to jump into another relationship as a safety patch to help you cope with the difficult feelings you're having;

- It's not a good idea to try and distract yourself from the problem at hand - it's better to face it head on, no matter how upsetting or difficult it is;

- The future is brighter, even if it doesn't feel that way right now.

CONCLUSION

We've now come to the end of our book about divorcing a narcissist.

How do you feel now?

Do you feel well informed and confident that you're clear on the road ahead? Do you feel like you might be ready to take the first step towards initiating divorce proceedings? Have the contents of the book helped you to understand that none of this is your fault and that you're free to walk away?

We hope that you feel more positive at this stage. Whilst it's normal to feel sad at the same time, because you're about to end a marriage that you hoped would last you a lifetime, it's important to realize that you do not deserve to live your life in the grips of a narcissist and their constant manipulation and control.

You can set yourself free, and whilst the road ahead may not be smooth, it will come to an end and leave you with a brighter future ahead.

Divorce of any kind is messy and difficult. Choosing your divorce attorney carefully is vital. As we've mentioned several times throughout the book, choosing an attorney who has specific experience and deep knowledge of narcissism is important. In this case, they can help you to navigate everything that the narcissist may throw your way and help you to end the divorce with a fair result.

If you have children, remember that they must always come first. We obviously don't have to tell you this, but it's a point that's worth making. When a divorce takes hold, things can become overwhelming and when you add narcissism to the mix, it's even easier for the whole situation to turn very sour indeed.

All that's left to say is good luck.

Stay as positive as you can be, focus on the future, understand that whilst the road ahead may not be easy, it will be worthwhile in the end. Choose your attorney carefully, be sure of what you want, plan everything out, and seek support from those close to you. If you have to mend some broken bridges in order to build up your support network, don't be afraid to do so.

Life does not have to be controlled by a narcissist. You do not have to be manipulated and you do not have to live your life trying to please someone who will never be pleased.

Look to the future with hope and happiness will come your way.

If you enjoyed this book, please let me know your thoughts by leaving a short review on **Amazon**, it means a lot to me!

Thank you.